THE PILGRIMS
& THE PASSION

MESSAGES FOR LENT AND EASTER

GEORGE M. BASS

AUGSBURG PUBLISHING HOUSE
MINNEAPOLIS, MINNESOTA

THE PILGRIMS AND THE PASSION

Library of Congress Catalog Card No. 72-90256

International Standard Book No. 0-8066-1303-3

ACKNOWLEDGEMENTS

The publishers referred to in the list that follows kindly gave per-
mission to include in this volume material copyrighted in their
name.

From Random House, Inc.
  Real People, by Alison Lurie, Copyright © 1969

From Alfred A. Knopf, Inc.
  The Devil with Love, by Robert Nathan, Copyright © 1963
  "The Crooked Man" from *We Have Seen the Best of Our Times,*
  by Nancy Potter, Copyright © 1969

From Simon and Schuster, Inc.
  Up the Sandbox, by Anne Richardson Roiphe, Copyright © 1971
  A Measure of Dust, by Steven Turner, Copyright © 1970

From Stein and Day/Publishers
  The Way of an Eagle, by Dan Potter, Copyright © 1969 by
  Dan Potter

CONTENTS

To the memory of my parents
Harry and Ruth Bass

and for my parents through marriage
Albert and Walber Haggarty

I must acknowledge the part my wife, Doris, played in this project by her willing participation in pilgrimages to Jerusalem and Rome, and for sharing ideas, books, and passages with me from her "Roman-winter reading program."

THE PILGRIMS AND THE PASSION

Lent is the time of the year when faithful Christians participate in a pilgrimage to Jerusalem. This is more than a penitential period leading to a time of temporary joy in the Easter Eucharist; it is a dynamic and moving experience, with lasting effects, for the people of God. Lent invites concentration upon the remembrance of Jesus' death and resurrection—his Passion—while demanding that this redeeming event be related to the great issues of life: the alienation of humanity from itself and God; the engulfing shadows of selfishness so evident in modern life; godless materialism and preoccupation with the pursuit of pleasure; pride of race and nation; the obvious lack of love for God, others, and self; the unwillingness of Christians to live as though Jesus is really the Lord—the "gap" between the faith professed and the life that is lived. Man, living in a world threatened with ultimate and final destruction, needs a word of hope—deliverance and direction—from God.

Lenten preaching, informed by the Passion of Christ, on one hand, and by the needs of people and their world, on the other, draws upon the experience and pattern of the past, which reveals that such preaching was didactic, devotional, and penitential. The setting was basically sacramental with the Easter Eucharist as the climactic and pivotal experience. Today, sermons in Lent ought to encourage devotion, inspire the study of scripture, initiate reflection and meditation that, through the Holy Spirit, will turn men toward the Risen Lord and the new life he offers to all. In public worship, preaching should contribute to an immediate experience of God's love and grace in the gospel, and to the rebuilding of broken lives and a shattered world. What is said in the pulpit needs to be supplemented by other public and private devotional activities—frequent celebration of the Eucharist, daily devotions with prayer, reading, study, and thought about the Word of God, plus the use of the rich resources of music, drama, literature, and the other arts—as these enrich the "going up to Jerusalem" and the ever-continuing pilgrimage of the Christian life.

The "Songs of Ascents"—Psalms 120 to 134—are the "pilgrim hymns" inherited by the Christian Church from the Hebrews, who sang them on their way to Jerusalem to celebrate the Passover. In themselves, they provide preachers with a biblical basis for preaching on Lent as a Christian pilgrimage. Their spirit is reflected in the gospels, as, for example, when Jesus says, "Behold, we go up to Jerusalem . . . ;" they—Jesus and the disciples—

undoubtedly sang and prayed these Psalms as they traveled to the Holy City. Many of the themes find parallel expression and pertinent expansion in the Sermon on the Mount, where the Lord laid out a route for pilgrims to follow in this world. Some of the Psalms are more meaningful today than others; sometimes, only a "key" verse speaks to the situation and needs of pilgrims of the 20th century; and these help to shape the sermons which follow.

The Sermon on the Mount is the primary source for THE PILGRIMS AND THE PASSION. It reveals a way of life—in the kingdom God initiated in Jesus Christ—that is rich and satisfying, but costly. Put in the framework of Lent, Jesus' idealistic plan for humanity seems doomed at the cross—and, today, total annihilation of the world, as predicted by an ever-growing number of people, could be the final act in that drama that began in Jerusalem —at Calvary and in a garden. The Sermon on the Mount offers a paradox to the preacher in that Jesus, who wouldn't compromise by changing to another "route" in life, had to die on the cross, while we, who hesitate to follow his pattern for life, so that our lives are almost a continual compromise with the gospel, are destroying life itself. These sermons are meant to speak to that paradox, looking to the Good Friday-Easter Event for resolution that will result in the rebirth of hope and new life in the world.

The pilgrimage of our Lord took place between the mountain on which he preached and the one from which he ascended. There he lived out, among real people whose problems were as real as ours, what he taught in his "sermon." His death on an ugly little hill between the mountains verifies what he said, and his resurrection renews the import of his teachings. He, as God's Word to man, revealed in Pilgrimage and Passion, is the personal goal of the pilgrims who keep Lent. Lent speaks for him and gathers his people in perpetual pilgrimage, saying, "Follow me—to the cross and empty tomb —and to life!"

Psalm 122:1, 2

> How I rejoiced when they said to me,
> 'Let us go to the house of Yahweh!'
> And now our feet are standing
> in your gateways, Jerusalem.

Matthew 20:17-19

> Jesus was going up to Jerusalem, and on the way he took the Twelve to one side and said to them, 'Now we are going up to Jerusalem, and the Son of Man is about to be handed over to the chief priests and the scribes. They will condemn him to death and will hand him over to the pagans to be mocked and scourged and crucified; and on the third day he will rise again.'

Read also: Luke 18:34; Matthew 5:1, 2, and 10.

1.

THE PILGRIMS AND THE PASSION

Lent is the annual pilgrimage of the people of God. It is a very different sort of journey; we are not "led by a star," as at Jesus' birth, but we are *drawn by a cross* to Jerusalem—and Calvary. We keep Lent to recall Jesus' death—all the callous details of it—and that makes it—our pilgrimage—a grim sort of trip. We choke up a bit when we try to say, or sing, the ancient song of the Israelites as they went up to Jerusalem to celebrate the Passover:

> How I rejoiced when they said to me,
>   'Let us go to the house of Yahweh!'
> And now our feet are standing
>   in your gateways, Jerusalem.

Who dares to be a Christian pilgrim bound for Jerusalem, knowing what we know of the death of the Lord? Who can rejoice at the invitation to "go up to Jerusalem," even when it comes from the Lord himself? "Let us go up . . ." is really a command from the Christ contained in his announcement, "Now we are going up to Jerusalem, and the Son

11

of Man . . . (will be) crucified. . . . " The promise in his postscript to the prophesy doesn't help much, ". . . and on the third day he will rise again." The cross is not pleasant to contemplate!

The Passion demands a reaction

Matthew's account of Jesus' announcement of his impending suffering and death is puzzling. He records no reaction! And this is the third time that Jesus tells the disciples of his Passion and death. Luke, at least, excuses them: "But they could make nothing of this; what he said was quite obscure to them, they had no idea what he meant." Maybe that's why they did nothing. Maybe that's why they didn't attempt to debate the journey with him. Maybe that's the reason they didn't attempt to dissuade him, or revert to physical force to deter him from going to Jerusalem—and certain death. Had they understood, they certainly would have done something to spare him the pain of the Passion.

Three young girls, who lived in Sicily, were murdered on their way home from school one day by the deranged uncle of two of the girls. Their parents were away from home seeking employment when the tragedy occurred. On their return home, the grieving father drove out to the site where the bodies had been discovered. A group of men was there, continuing the investigation into the deaths. When they recognized the man in the "mini" car, they quickly walked over to it, picked it up and turned it completely around in the opposite direction so that the father couldn't even see the site that had given up their broken bodies. Jesus' "now we are going up . . . " might have initiated similar action by the disciples—at least an attempt to dissuade the beloved Lord from going, or an urgent plea, "be careful! Don't take any chances in Jerusalem." But they obeyed—and went with him, saying or doing nothing.

We know—or think we do—what we would have done! Conditioned by an age of confrontation, we would have insisted that there has to be another way to "save the world." A few of us might have been bold enough to tell him, "Don't take yourself so seriously, Jesus; you can't really save the world," much in the manner of Judas' pitiful plea in *Jesus Christ Superstar*, remembering what he had said long ago:

> The spirit of the Lord has been given to me,
> for he has anointed me.
> He has sent me to bring the good news to the poor,
> to proclaim liberty to captives
> and to the blind new sight,
> to set the downtrodden free,
> to proclaim the Lord's year of favour.
> (Luke 4:18-19)

Some of us would have urged, "Stay out of Jerusalem, Lord—and the danger of death!" But nothing would have stopped him—then, or now.

The dilemma pilgrims face

Why should we become pilgrims during Lent when we already know Jesus' fate in the Holy City? The story is as familiar as it is tragic. And nothing

really seems to have changed in the nearly 20 centuries since his crucifixion. Mankind still does all the
inhuman deeds—murder, war, stealing, lying, rape,
and other forms of hate and evil—that were familiar
to Jesus and his contemporaries. The Chinese Com-
munists were really criticizing Christianity—and the
cross—when they announced one Christmas, "There
is no 'peace on earth.' " His life and death seem to
have been futile when we survey the hatred and hos-
tility that afflict the whole world like an incurable
illness.

Jesus' death seems so senseless—not simply because it is the worst of humanity's heartless acts on
earth—but because we wonder what he hoped to
accomplish by dying on a cross. In a way, his death
is more puzzling than the resurrection. Man's hopes
for conquering death, for a larger life, even for a
new world, are comprehended in the resurrection,
that eternal mystery, which as an actual event, is
totally incomprehensible to the human mind. Death
—the terrible termination of physical life—is our constant and common enemy which, sooner or later,
takes its toll in everyone's life. Death, that unwelcome guest, only becomes man's friend when the
pain of existence is too much to bear, or physical
suffering too much to tolerate. Death becomes a lib-
erator of the living when an evil man—a fiendish
ruler, a despotic dictator, or, maybe, a blood-letting
lunatic—is burned to ashes or buried in the ground.
When a good man dies—willingly sacrificing himself in a way that promises nothing that is of evident and immediate benefit to men and their world
—we wonder and weep in our dilemma.

Jesus was a solitary pilgrim

Why did Jesus begin that pilgrimage that had to end in his Passion and death? If not deluded, was he a fatalist who literally accepted the words of the prophets who lived hundreds of years before he was born? Was he too religious—something of a fanatic? Or did he see his death as a *warning* to the human race, as though this were the common fate that man could anticipate for his kind—and all life on earth? Did he really know what he was doing—and also believe that something perpetually beneficial to humanity would result when he said, "Let us go up . . . ?"

Jesus *was* the only one who really understood. He knew that "God was in . . . (his death), reconciling the world to himself," setting all things right—forever!—so he made the pilgrimage known as his Passion. And as we "go up to Jerusalem," we join that solitary Pilgrim, recalling his suffering and death in an attempt to comprehend more of, and participate more fully in, that mysterious action by which God "makes all things new." At Jesus' cross—and, then, at his empty tomb—God gathers all of his children together, and declares to them what Paul put into words: "I will tell you something that has been secret: that we are not all going to die, but we shall all be changed. . . . When this perishable nature has put on imperishability, and when this mortal nature has put on immortality, then the words of scripture will come true: *Death is swallowed up in victory. Death, where is your victory? Death, where is your sting?* . . . So let us thank God for giving us the victory through Jesus Christ our Lord." (1 Corinthians 15:51-57)

The ancient pilgrims' hymn, "I was glad when they said unto me, Let me go to the house of the Lord"—to Jerusalem and the cross—has new meaning for the Christian pilgrims, who add:

> Now thank we all our God,
> With hearts and hands and voices;
> Who wondrous things hath done,
> In Whom his world rejoices.

For God's glory and loving grace shine through the Passion of his Son's humble and complete obedience at the cross.

Pilgrims perceive the purpose of the Passion

Lent is our approach to the cross, our turn, as pilgrims, to go up to Jerusalem with the Lord. For some, it may be the first time; for others, it may be the 50th time they have made the pilgrimage. But it is crucial to all. Life, not just death, hangs in the balance, for those who take that road. No one who hears "Now we are going up to Jerusalem . . ." can hold back on the grounds that he has heard the story —been that way—before. Something awful in this world is trying to crush the life out of us—every day —and without the victorious combination of death and resurrection which we find at the end of the trip on Good Friday and Easter, life might not be worth living at all. Pilgrims, who keep Lent, perceive the purpose of the Passion, through the grace of God. Those who share in the "fellowship of his suffering" are offered God's fantastic gift for living, "the power of his resurrection."

God's gifts to people—mental power, physical beauty and strength, charismatic personalities, and multi-faceted talents—seldom seem to be disturbed evenly among the human race. A minority received more—or less, too—than the majority of mankind. We envy—even appreciate—the truly gifted, possibly wondering why they have more gifts than we do. John Evelyn, during a visit to Rome in the 17th century, recorded in his diary that Giovanni Bernini, whose great gifts as an architect and sculptor are so well known—he developed techniques in carving marble whereby he was able to reproduce accurately the differences in texture between flesh, silk, feathers, and clouds—had additional gifts. Bernini "gave an opera wherein he painted the scenery, carved the statues, invented the machinery (to move scenery and props), composed the music, wrote the comedy, and built the theatre." Few men have gifts and talents in such abundance, but the gift of gifts, life—the power really to hope and live—God freely gives to any man, to every man.

Christian pilgrims may be bold to follow Christ to Jerusalem again—and to encourage others to take part in the pilgrimage we know as Lent—for God will renew that gift at the cross and the garden tomb. The procession of the pilgrims is about to begin again. Let us join the line of march and follow the route to Jerusalem, the Passion, and life.

Psalm 123:1

I lift my eyes to you
to you who have your home in heaven, . . .

Matthew 6:19-21

'Do not store up treasures for yourselves on earth, where moths and woodworms destroy them and thieves can break in and steal. But store up treasures for yourselves in heaven, where neither moth nor woodworm destroy them and thieves cannot break in and steal. For where your treasure is, there will your heart be also.

Read also: Matthew 6:16-18, 22-24.

2.

PILGRIMS HAVE
PRIORITIES

The Lenten pilgrimage is *a way to life,* the life of a new world and an age to come—through Jesus' death and resurrection. It also has to do with *a way of life,* God's plan for mankind on the earth. The first requires a deep devotional life of Christian pilgrims during their lenten journey; the second brings into focus the penitential aspects of the Christian life, insisting that the children of God examine the quality of their lives and their priorities in life. They are brought together—as they should be—in this traditional Ash Wednesday Gospel from the Sermon on the Mount.

*Heaven and earth—contrasting and
conflicting priorities*

Two contemporary organizations—one secular and the other sacred—received world-wide publicity in the same issue of *Time* (January 24, 1972), only six pages apart. The secular organization is the Club

19

of Rome, whose purpose is to explore "the large issues confronting society." It was organized in 1968 by Aurelio Peccei, an Italian economist and former president of the Olivetti firm, because "We needed something to make mankind's predicament more viable, more easy to grasp." The Club of Rome has been described as prestigious, with a membership list of important scientists, economists, manufacturers, political leaders—70 in all. Its concerns are strictly secular.

The other group was known as the Children of God. They are young people, hippies and fundamentalists, Christians who literally base their lives on the Bible. Richard Zahler wrote of them, "Their talk is hip, their music is rock, but their names and the daily acts of their lives are taken from literal reading and adaptation of the Bible. They," he continues, "profess to live like the earliest Christians." The Children of God had renounced the world, lived in communes in the United States and around the world in the belief that Christ's second coming is imminent. Their fellowship included young people who have run away from home, reformed drug addicts, and a small cross section of modern youth. They emphasized the devotional aspects of Christianity, allowing three hours a day for work, two hours for meals (breakfast and supper), and three hours of unassigned time for "personal chores such as laundry and Bible memorization. The rest of the day between 8 A.M. and midnight was devoted to structured religious activity—classes, group workshop periods, and . . . revival-like inspiration hours." Their reason for existence was avowedly religious.

The Club of Rome and the Children of God, at the time of publication, held one conviction in common—humanity is heading for a crisis that threatens it with extinction. The "Children" called it "doomsday," and find its description in the Bible. The Club of Rome, as the result of a computer study made by Dennis Meadows, concludes that "the depletion of non-renewable resources will probably cause the end of the civilization enjoyed by today's contented consumer." But while both organizations envision an "end to the world," if in slightly different ways and terminology, they immediately part company. The Children of God were preparing to "go to Heaven"—that was their priority in life—but the Club of Rome has—as their priority and purpose— an attempt to save humanity from self-destruction; they want to preserve the earth for mankind and all life. The "Children" used the Bible in their quest; the "Club" employs the sciences, computers, and common sense to reach their conclusion: "A series of fundamental shifts in behavioral patterns must take place. Instead of yearning for material goods, people must learn to prefer services, like education or recreation." *Time's* unidentified reporter concludes: "One glaring weakness remains in the report (of Meadows for the Club of Rome). It lacks a description of how a society dedicated to upward and onward growth can change its ways." The *Time* religion reporter raised a crucial question about the Children of God—"whether they are prepared to live more fully in the world if doomsday does not come as expected." Lent—its pilgrimage—causes us to question both sets of priorities, particularly as they find expression in each of us.

Lent orders the priorities of pilgrims

Long ago, one man spoke to the problem of man's priorities and put them in proper perspective at the very beginning of his ministry. Jesus' "Do not store up treasures for yourselves on earth. . . . But store up treasures for yourselves in heaven . . ." seems to support the heaven-oriented stance of the Children of God, rejecting the earth-intentions of the Club of Rome. But this is not necessarily so. Christ wasn't pitting heaven—and eternal life—against the earth—with its physical and temporal existence; he was actually probing more deeply into man's priorities, getting at the root of man's problem—the nature of his love and how it is oriented.

The concern for heaven and the preoccupation with the hereafter—to the exclusion of fulfilling the responsibilities of love in this life—can be the result of concern about, and love for, self. Efforts to preserve and save life on the earth may be—if they spring from honest and generous intentions—more religious than those of people who give up on the earth and simply want to go to heaven. Jesus came to put both types of priorities in the perspective of sacrificial love for God and man. Lent—through his Passion—helps us to see this.

In Robert Nathan's novel, *The Devil with Love,* there is an episode in which Father Deener, a Catholic priest, attempts to exorcise the evil spirit from Samuel of Hod, who is in the employ of Satan.

He fails; the ancient liturgy avails nothing. Samuel tells him, "It is beautiful, Father, . . . but it is use- less. It is too old-fashioned: it belongs to a more innocent time in history, when good and evil were easily separated into black and white. It is not so simple any more." Father Deener could only bow his head and say, "I know." And Samuel proceeds to point out that man has pulled down the walls of faith and love that were around him and has created his own hell on earth.

He continues: "He has learned much; he stands today upon the very threshold of the great mys- teries. But they will not make him innocent again, or fill him with that grace which gave his spirit strength, or make him happy. Of all the gifts given him at the beginning, what has he left? Tell me."

Silent for a moment, Father Deener spoke "in a low voice," at last: "He has the gift of love."

"Yes," said Samuel slowly, "he has the gift of love. But can he love beyond himself?"

And this is the question that is at the root of our problem with priorities in our lives and our world. The Passion of the Lord re-orders them through Jesus' gracious gospel and life of love and sacrifice.

Lent is always a time of self-examination

Pilgrims move by the Spirit of the Lord and live the life of worship and devotion. They "go up to Jerusalem" by prayer, as well as hearing and read- ing the Word of God. Lent is at once the time when we anticipate the Passion again, but it is equally the period when we assess our own priorities and the basis on which they have been established. Ultimately, we pilgrims have to face up to questions we like to dodge, but which, when fully resolved, open up "the gates to new life," as James S. Stewart has put it. Some of the questions are: "Do I really *love* the Lord God I say I believe in?" Is Jesus really the Lord of my life?" "Do I honestly care about my fellowman and the world we live in—beyond myself and my own little world?" And, finally, "What am *I* doing to help save people and their world?"

The pilgrimage of the people of God during Lent concerns the best of two worlds, heaven and earth, time and eternity. The journey to the cross and tomb is best negotiated by believers whose hearts and minds are fixed on the things of God, but whose feet are firmly planted in the soil of earthly life. They reject a one-track faith, oriented to concerns for either heaven or earth which are mutually exclusive. In that one mighty event, spanning life, death, and eternity, the seemingly contradictory priorities of our time—all time—are brought together to our temporal and eternal benefit. Through Jesus and his Passion we discover that we can love beyond ourselves—and when we love God first and our neighbor as ourselves, our priorities fall into proper sequence and result—on our part—in effective and redeeming action in the world.

Psalm 125:1

Those who trust in Yahweh are like Mount Zion,
unshakeable, standing for ever.

Matthew 5:17, 20

'Do not imagine that I have come to abolish
the Law or the Prophets. I have come not to
abolish but to complete them.—For I tell you,
if your virtue goes no deeper than that of the
scribes and Pharisees, you will never get into
the kingdom of heaven.'

Read also: Matthew 5:21-26

3.

THE PILGRIM LIFE IS A PASSIONATE JOURNEY

The Christian life is a passionate journey. The followers of Jesus Christ, true to the nature of the gospel, have a genuinely profound love for the Lord and a dynamic concern for other people which are expressed in every area of life. Those who love the Lord—and being Christian asserts this—exhibit in their relationships and service to the world the same quality of love and passion that marks their expressions of praise and thanksgiving to God. Pilgrims are sensitized to the passionate nature of life by the nature of Jesus' Passion as it unfolds so fully during Lent.

Contemporary conditions call for passionate living

In her *Up the Sandbox,* Anne Richardson Roiphe relates a series of imaginary incidents in the life of a young housewife, a member of the Women's Liberation Movement; she lives in New York City. Her heroine promotes and participates passionately in all sorts of service projects—most of them revolutionary in nature—while her college professor husband is occupied in writing a well-documented, scholarly book that expounds a thesis for life that is diametrically opposed to hers. He insists that history proves that violent revolutions fall short of their goals and become evil, destructive. One night, just before she goes to sleep—after a miserable evening in which they clashed over their opposing philosophies—she thinks: ". . . I had one final thought about his book. I won't tell him, as he would find me absurd, but I'm certain that, despite historical evidence, revolutions must take place and one day one of them will be led by a real hero who will neither sell out his cause nor find himself knifed in the back. Some day there will be a revolution with genuine heroes and the way of life for that country will change and the air will be clean. If I don't believe in that possibility, then I see only total destruction ahead, as one power after another fights and destroys, ultimately killing us all."

The ever-enlarging community of alert and concerned people today, genuinely interested in the deteriorating and crisis-ridden estate of the human race, also believes that the times call for passionate action, as well as deep concern. Radical change is mandatory to rescue man and save his world; nearly everybody is aware of that. Revolution, as a form of passionate living, is vigorously promoted as a method of change that is more immediate and effective than anything else. Many have abandoned the gospel—and the Christian Church—because living the

Passion doesn't seem to affect much change in society.

Pilgrims live the Passion

The Passion of the Lord also calls for passionate living, but of a kind not seen frequently enough in the world. Christ has been called a revolutionary leader, but, if so, he is a very different sort of leader than many persons make him out. The problem seems to be that, in our passionate zeal, it is very simple to leave the cross out of his life and message, proceeding on a "love one another before it is too late," or a "love is enough" basis for living passionately. And when we reduce the gospel this way, we change it for the worse.

Dan Potter's hero, Buddy Sumday, in *The Way of an Eagle*, is a man of his times who has dedicated himself to a kind of passionate journey with Jesus Christ. He drove into a small town on a white motorcycle—with a black dove painted on each side of the gas tank—and stopped at a gasoline station whose proprietor, Harry Frinlee, was waiting on a customer dressed in a military uniform. Harry thought that the hippies had finally discovered his town, and he feared the worst when the young man removed his helmet and revealed long, unruly hair. But then he grinned, disarmingly, and held out his hand to Harry:

"Buddy Sumday, he said, No past, no future, just a present for you" (and he withdrew a Gideon Bible from his jacket and handed it to Harry. Then, looking at the customer, Dick White, son of the local clergyman and a Vietnam veteran suffering from "battle fatigue," he dug into a pocket and found a plastic flower which he gave him. A brief verbal encounter resulted and Dick threw down the flower, got into his car and crushed it with his wheels as he drove out of the gas station. Buddy picked up the smashed flower, looked at it, and put it in a waste can. Then he pointed at the Bible, as he turned to Harry, and asked:)

"You gonna throw that away?"

"Why—uh—no, I (Harry is the story-teller) said."

"Good. We love Him, because He first loved us. John 4:19. You a religious man, Harry?"

"Well I'm a Christian."

"Didn't ask you that. You love God?"

"Well, sure I do. I guess."

"A guess is as good as a miss, and a miss is as good as a mile. You love *me?*"

". . . you could've knocked me over with a feather. I heard him all right, but I was still standin' there with my tongue hangin' out when he said,

"It's all right, Harry. Don't be embarrassed. The Good Book says to greet one another with a holy kiss, but we're not quite ready for that yet—I mean all of us. So, let's get down to business. . . . "

Buddy's immediate business was asking Harry for a chance to show what he could do around the service station in the hope of obtaining a permanent job. He also wanted to settle down in the town and live as he believed a Christian should live; he, too, was a veteran of Vietnam and he wanted to contribute to humanity by helping to change the world. But Buddy's brand of Christianity was strictly contemporary, really sub-gospel, despite his facile and continual use of biblical quotations. His life-style was indeed passionate, but he was hardly living the Passion-oriented life of Christ. His very contemporaneity so dominated his passion and life that it gave a strange twist to the gospel and to his expressions of concern for the people he encountered. In the end, a length of chain and a brutal beating by three of the people he tried to help hospitalized him, terminating his activities in that place. He disappeared from the hospital one night as mysteriously as he had appeared there—on his white motorcycle; his passion for people had not been enough to sustain him and his mission in life. His version of the passionate life of the gospel had no cross in it, and when he left, nothing had really changed in the town. Christians—pilgrims—have to live the Passion, but not on their own terms—on God's.

The Passion is the pattern for passionate living

Pilgrims discover the true pattern for the passionate, the Christian life in the recapitulation during Lent of Jesus' pilgrimage to the cross. His cross not only sensitizes us to the needs of people in the world and motivates us to do what we can to help our brothers, but it teaches us that our lives, as truly passionate Christians, follow the pattern of the cross. That's why Lent is an experience that explodes through Word and Spirit any spark of life and love within us into a flame that burns brightly and passionately. It ignites in us a love for God and a useful life on earth. If less than this, Lent is only waiting for Easter, and life is but the expectation of death—to which the hope of heaven has been added.

The cross has a way of stopping us in our tracks, causing us to ponder and wonder about the depth of Jesus' Passion so that we respond "My Lord and my God." But coupled to his death and resurrection, as well, the emerging pattern for the passionate life of the pilgrim is that of an active goodness; we can't stand before the cross—however devotional and holy our attitude—and call that Christian discipleship, the passionate life of the gospel.

Natalie MacFee, a minister's wife in Nancy Potter's story, "The Crooked Man," is a person whose life was a round of routine and meaningless activities. Driven by an encounter with an acquaintance, an artist named Gatti, she visits him in his studio to continue their discussion. Gatti sees the emptiness of her existence and says to her: "It would be impossible to see you do anything significant to be hated for. You were sealed into a kind of paralyzed goodness. You know that, don't you? Neat as a paper clip. Virtue becomes you. It hangs on you like a shroud." He continues: "Some human beings never get used to being human. . . . So you're waiting around for some new life to begin."

Suddenly, Natalie has the kind of revelation that occurs when one begins to understand what Jesus was talking about when he said, "I have not come to destroy the Law or the Prophets . . . but to complete them. . . ." She understands what he meant, " . . . if your virtue goes no deeper than that of the scribes and the Pharisees . . . ," and answers Gatti: "I do what I have despised people for doing before this. I run over the possible horrors that we have avoided. That's why people take the daily newspapers. To be superior. To say, we didn't do that. At least we haven't fallen completely apart. We didn't get drunk enough to drive the car into a school bus or become shoplifters in the meat market or get multiple sclerosis or gain two hundred pounds. If you do nothing, you avoid all of these." After a pause, she asks him the unspoken question of the cross and Passion, "What have you done?" She was at the point where the rays of the gospel were beginning to penetrate her empty world of "self" and sterile holiness and was on the verge of becoming an intelligent and dedicated disciple of the Lord. Before her a new road for life had opened up—a possible passionate journey.

That way—our living the pattern created by his Passion—is set before us in his consuming desire to "complete the Law and the Prophets" and, thereby, ". . . finish the work that the Father has given me to do." That way is the way of the cross, the gospel of God's love for the world—God's word of hope for humanity. And that cross, set before his empty tomb, is both the culmination—and the beginning—of our passionate journey for God and our fellow man.

Psalm 128:1

Happy, all those who fear Yahweh
and follow in his paths.

Matthew 5:20, 21

'You have learnt how it was said to our ancestors: . . . But I say this to you: . . . '

Reread: Matthew 5:17-26; read also: Matthew
5:27-48

4.

PILGRIMS FOLLOW A
DIFFICULT PATH

Two couples, one Jewish and the other Christian, were discussing travel experiences during lunch one day. They also discussed future travel plans—trips they wanted to take. The Christian couple mentioned that they had been to Israel and wanted to go there again, at which the Jewish man registered complete surprise and asked, "Why?" The Christians told him that their trip to the Holy Land was one of the great experiences of their lives. They had planned it—and taken it—as tourists, but it developed into a religious happening which changed them into pilgrims. Before the visit was finished, they found themselves agreeing that Mohammed's great exhortation about it, spoken before his disenchantment with Jews and Christians: "It is the land of God's great ingathering. Go and worship in it, for one act of worship is worth 10,000 elsewhere." Toward the end of the conversation, the Jewish man said, almost wistfully, "I'd go to Israel tomorrow, if I thought it would turn me into a religious person." He wanted

God to work some kind of instantaneous miracle—
painless and cost-free—and change him into a person
of faith, a new and different creature.

More than a few Christians approach Lent and its
pilgrimage with similar—if unspoken—thoughts and
emotions about Lent. They—perhaps all of us—want
something important and impressive to happen to
us that will warm and deepen our faith. We desire
to feel the power of God during Lent, working upon
us as, according to Archbishop George Appleton of
Jerusalem, the Old City affects even contemporary,
secular Jews. He says that they suddenly find their
"Jewishness welling up unexpectedly . . . as they
stand before the Western (Wailing) Wall." And
Lent does not disappoint faithful Christians—pilgrims—who are prepared through God's Word to
stand before Christ's tree and tomb.

Lent offers no easy road to pilgrims

The Jewish man would seem to have a better
opportunity to have a religious experience than the
pilgrim who seeks to keep Lent; he needs to do but
little beyond making the journey to Jerusalem,
where the place and history will take over. For the
Christian pilgrim, things are more difficult and
complicated; he stays where he is, lives in his usual
culture, and does things with which he is already
familiar—worships and prays, reads the Bible, thinks,
and imagines. For him, Lent is an exercise in awareness—a revelation about the reality of a loving God
who offers people the true way of life in his Son.
Unfortunately, there is no easy way to go, and stand

before, the cross of Christ and, thereby, become a really religious person in Lent. The road the pilgrim takes is difficult.

Pilgrims have to reckon with the teachings of Jesus—if they desire to become more aware of God and his ways—as well as proceed to the cross. Jesus didn't simply go to his death on Calvary as a form of protest or demonstration. His life and teachings—the expression of his deep faith in the Father—were connected to the cross; God's holy Law, which men could not keep, led him to Golgotha—and death, sacrificial and atoning. He got into trouble with the authorities partly because he added depth and dimension to the Law, by his life and his words, thereby complicating the lives of his followers—but revealing the secret of genuine awareness as well.

The people in the Lincoln Square Synagogue, in Manhattan, have been experiencing something of a revival, which is occurring through their study of the Law of God. Rabbi Steven Risk ministers to the descendants of people who plodded through the ghettos of the cities of the world, to survivors of the Nazi concentration camps and their offspring and relatives, to people whose whole history has been marked by suffering, enslavement and an on-going struggle for freedom, and he insists that the Law of God is relevant and vital today. "A God," he says, "who loves must give commands, must be concerned about the way His people live." By making their synagogue a place of study, a "community of the concerned" is being formed, their lives shaped by a real encounter with God's Word for faithful service.

Jesus takes us beyond the literal limits of the Law: "You have learnt how it was said to our ancestors: (You must not kill, . . . commit adultery, . . . love your neighbor and hate your enemy—etc.) but I say to you. . . ." And this is what makes life so difficult for the pilgrims.

People want Jesus—but not his way

Most of Jesus' reinterpretations of the Law seem impractical to contemporary people. It is just too much to expect people to equate anger with murder, or to "love their enemies," or to "pluck out your eye" or "cut off your hand if it offends you." The Sermon on the Mount, with its new standards of morality and ethics for the Christian life, belongs to Jesus' era, not ours, as far as many contemporary people are concerned.

Alison Laurie recently wrote a novel which she titled *Real People*. Her story is about a country estate, Illyria, which has been endowed by a wealthy woman as a retreat for artists. The painters, sculptors, composers, writers, poets, and other artists who go there to work have freedom from all of the things which complicate their lives and limit their work; most produce in a few days what it would take weeks, or months, to do at home. They become "real people"—for the retreat is almost an encounter group, sensitivity training, if you will—and they are different when they leave Illyria. Janet Belle Smith, a writer, is the chief character in the story, who becomes so liberated that she gets involved with a painter, Nick; her husband and children are tem-

porarily dismissed. Anne Roiphe's "liberated housewife" could have been speaking for Janet when she
questioned, "Is fidelity a virtue or a chain, a sign of
middle-class stupidity, an unthinking bourgeois reaction? or is it a lack of courage that keeps us couples
stuck to each other with occasional guilty thoughts
at midnight?" But Janet's experience is different;
she goes beyond limited liberation to the adoption
of a new way of life.

Janet Smith became so sensitized—to herself and
her career—that she became deliberately insensitive
to others when she became a "real person." She
thought, ". . . Lovely Janet doesn't really exist and
never did. . . . Lovely Janet didn't really write very
well—she left too much out. She didn't want to
depress her readers. She didn't want to make them
uncomfortable. She didn't want to expose her family, her friends, or (above all) herself; she didn't
want them to be laughed at, or pitied or condemned
—not even when they were in fact ridiculous, piti-
able and wrong." She concludes: "You can't write
well with only the nice parts of your character, and
only about nice things. And I don't want to try any
more. I want to use everything, including hate and
envy and lust and fear." And she adds, "Not only
do I want to—I must."

Enough evidence exists to support the conclusion
that untold numbers of people—including church
people who want to be modern and haven't measured
their values by Law and Gospel—have adopted this
sort of moral, ethical, and religious—or non-religious
—stance. But Jesus says to the pilgrim, to every
Christian, "But *I* say to you. . . ."

Why the pilgrim's road has to be difficult

When God's Law is taken seriously, it always causes men to throw themselves upon the mercy of God; who can fully comprehend it, let alone observe it? It is the necessary prelude to honest confession of need and forgiveness, imperative for us and our world. In the Law, we learn true awareness of God, real sensitivity to others and self, and come to understand why Christ and the cross were—still are—necessary.

Saul Amron is an anthropologist, created by Paule Marshall in *The Chosen Place, the Timeless People,* who believes that anthropologists must assist the people whose cultures they study, if they are true to their profession. With the support of his wife, Harriet, he goes to a Caribbean island and begins a research project there. Harriet and Saul seem to be well-matched and in love; she helps him in his work. In time, almost without warning, Saul drifts into a relationship with another woman, and Harriet, when she learns about it, panics, arranging through influential friends to have Saul "promoted" and sent back to Philadelphia. She wants to forgive and forget. But Saul, thoroughly professional in his work, has recurring problems in his personal life—he destroys nearly all those he loves—is furious when he learns what Harriet has done. He declares, "I am through with you . . . ," and storms out of their home. Harriet is later seen going to the beach for a swim—and is never seen again. And Saul? His stunned attitude speaks eloquently, "I never thought. . . ." Once more he had miserably failed someone he loved—and he didn't really know why. The Law, especially with Christ's interpretation attached to it, helps us see our need of forgiveness, grace and love—our need of Christ and the cross.

The other reason that the road which pilgrims travel in Lent is rough is that we need to realize how much we need the new life in Christ to have any hope of obeying his commands. The way of life he proclaimed is difficult for all, but impossible for those who try to obey the Law of God without his help. When at Good Friday and Easter we die and rise with him, we learn that with him everything is possible—even becoming his kind of real people, honestly aware of and loving God and man and self. Suddenly then, the difficult pilgrim-road we have been traveling becomes smooth and easy!

Psalm 121:1, 2

> I lift my eyes to the mountains
> where is help to come from?
> Help comes to me from Yahweh,
> who made heaven and earth.

Matthew 6:5

> 'And when you pray. . . .'

> Read also: Matthew 6:5-15; Matthew 7:7-11

5.

PILGRIMS PRAY AS THEY GO

A TV documentary program was recently produced and broadcast about the operation of a modern fishing fleet in the Mediterranean Sea. When the first ship was ready to sail, the crew gathered on deck. One man produced a medium-sized plastic bag containing a powder-like substance—it could have been grated cheese or sugar—said a few words and sprinkled the powder over the fishing nets. Next, a bottle of wine was brought out and held up, and a toast for good luck was said—and repeated —as the bottle was passed from man to man. That done, they returned to their posts and went to sea. No vested priest was there to invoke God's blessing on the venture; no public prayers were voiced for a safe return or anything else. They had a good, well-equipped ship; they just needed luck. And most of the sailor-fishermen were probably Christians; they not only failed to pray, but they didn't even make the sign of the cross. They could be representative of what has been called "the new breed of Christians" almost anywhere on earth.

Henry E. Horn, in his book *Worship in Crisis,* writes: "For centuries it was always assumed that daily praise, Scripture reading, and prayer would be the normal activity of Christians—their regular natural breathing within the kingdom of God." The pattern was established by the Hebrews, long before Jesus was born. Therefore, at the beginning of his ministry, he addressed people where they were, simply saying, "When you pray . . ."—not "You must pray. . . ." He would have to start differently today, if Horn is correct in his assessment: "Certainly all Christians, individually, are conscious that they have not been able to keep up private practices of praise, reading, and prayer . . . ; and we have asked his forgiveness often." The question is this: why don't we pray?

The same old question—why pray?

A Measure of Dust, a novel by Steven Turner, is the story of a few weeks in the life of a 13 year old boy, Mark Torrance, who attends a church-related school in Mississippi. At the end of the year, Mark is excused from examinations, sent home for a week by the headmaster—purportedly as a reward for being an honor student but really to dun his parents for back tuition they owe for Mark and his brother. He has to hitch-hike, because he has no money for bus fare.

Turner seems to be poking fun at religion, in general, prayer, in particular, when Mark is given a short ride by a famous evangelist—a Mr. Lance Godbold—who is well-known but nearly penniless. Mr. Godbold lives in an old shack; when they get there, he invites Mark, a deeply religious boy, into the house to join in prayer for his dying child. A doctor is coming out the door; he turns out to be Mr. Godbold's brother, and he later tells Mark that the baby, born three months' prematurely, has underdeveloped lungs.

Mr. Godbold said, "I've brought a boy to pray, Tom."

"You have, huh? Well, it's too bad you couldn't bring an oxygen tent."

Mr. Godbold shook his head slowly. "We don't need that. God is the great physician."

The doctor put (a) cigarette in his mouth. "Well, I'm not God and neither are you—no matter what you may think."

Mr. Godbold said, "Will you pray with us, Tom?"

The doctor shook his head. "I'd rather smoke."

"But, . . . maybe you'll at least wait and give this boy a ride . . . with you. He'll be leaving as soon as we finish praying."

. . . Then the doctor nodded. "I'll wait for him out on the porch. But don't let the prayer last longer than the cigarette."

They prayed—over a child whose breathing was labored and rapid—and, later, the doctor told Mark that the baby could not possibly live, even in a hospital. The power of prayer was forcefully and effectively put down. Or so it seemed. Turner's message seems to be "Prayer is useless. Why pray?"

46

Pilgrims are praying people

Pilgrims pray as they go, because pilgrims—informed and dedicated Christians—are praying people. They know who God is and what he has done; they don't need to test his power or his strength, thus they pray regularly—their prayers voice their gratitude, express their praise, confess their needs, and show their concern for the people who inhabit God's world. James Montgomery describes it poetically:

> Prayer is the Christian's native breath,
> The Christian's vital air. . . .

Pilgrims learn this from their Master.

The church at the bend of the road, overlooking the beautiful Mediterranean Sea, was almost empty —despite the fact that two tour buses were outside. The sounds of worship and prayer heard as the church was entered were mysterious; only a couple of women cleaning the nave were visible inside. A first reaction was that the church had provided a recording as atmosphere for visitors, but it soon became apparent that the voices were emanating from below the nave. Investigation revealed a crypt, obviously older than the building above it, and containing the sarcophagus of a young girl, a saint. Seventy or eighty people, led by two priests, were worshiping there. They were pilgrims—Polish pilgrims—1000 miles from home, part of a group of 5000 Poles—all pilgrims—who were in Rome to participate in "the making of a saint," a Polish priest and martyr. Their activities in this church were part of their pilgrimage, for they were not merely tourists. Prayer is a normal and natural activity of pilgrims; pilgrims always pray as they go.

Lent is the pilgrim's call to prayer

Our Lord's invitation, "Now we go up to Jerusalem," because it is an invitation to become pilgrims, is a behest to be—or become—praying people of God. It comes as the great *Venite:*

> Come, let us praise Yahweh joyfully,
> acclaiming the rock of our safety;
> let us come into his presence with thanksgiving,
> acclaiming him with music.
> For Yahweh is a great God,
> a greater King than all other gods;
> from depths of earth to mountain top
> everything comes under his rule;
> the sea belongs to him, he made it,
> so does the land, he shaped this too.
> Come in, let us bow, prostrate ourselves
> and kneel in front of Yahweh our maker,
> for this is our God,
> and we are the people he pastures,
> the flock that he guides.　　　(Psalm 98:1-7)

We know that our Redeemer who suffered and died on the cross lives and reigns with God, and that he listens to and answers every prayer. Our prayers—at all times, not just in Lent—must be *private,* as well as *public.* We have to explore all the different avenues of prayer during Lent, praying by ourselves "in our closet," with our families, and family-type groups, and with the larger Christian community to which we belong, in public worship. Pilgrims pray in groups of varying size, especially in Lent, but they pray. They know God and they know who they are his people, so they pray.

Pilgrim-Christian prayers are *precise* and *pertinent;* pilgrims know what prayer is all about. Pilgrims may use free prayers and formal prayers, but they never babble—whatever type of prayer they employ. Their prayers are informed by the Scriptures and by the needs of the world as well. The mind of individual pilgrim and the people of God is always in them; they have to be specific and relevant, meaningful to the Christian community, and acceptable to God.

Lent is the time when the prayers of the pilgrims increase in frequency and fervency so that they become *persistent* and *powerful.* God is real, alive, and active, even in an age of science and computer technology. He knows his own and supports them, just as he did his Son in the throes of his Passion and in the face of death. And this is really the message in Turner's *A Measure of Dust,* because, when Mark returns to pay his respects to Mr. Godbold and his wife after commencement at his school, he receives a surprise. The baby is still there, sleeping peacefully, breathing naturally—God has visited his people again, and Mark and the others learn a valuable lesson. Christ is the pilgrim's teacher and example in the business of prayer—and his is a living lesson in Lent—for every pilgrim.

The permanent pattern of pilgrim prayer

The Passion and cross teach us the ultimate facts we need to know about prayer; Jesus' "not my will, but thine be done" and his "My God, why . . .?" prayers were based on Scripture and, especially, the Prophets and Psalms. This is the combination that makes our prayers possible and practical; the Scriptures inform us and the Psalms inflame our imaginations even today!

At the Wailing Wall, one expects to see the old people swaying and praying; one is thrilled, but not surprised, by the Friday night gathering of the synagogues. But the schoolboys—10 or 11 years of age, Hasids with curls and conservative dress— reveal the secret behind the prayers of the Jewish community. They stand before the wall, sway rhythmically to the Psalms that they are reading, caught up as much as any teenager singing, dancing, or just listening to his rock music. They chant antiphonally—leader and group—and the Psalms become a litany of the faithful. They are pilgrims; they pray at the wall every day.

On the cross, Christ could not sway to the natural rhythm of the Psalms, but he could still pray in their words and spirit, "I lift my eyes to the mountains, where is help to come from. . . . " Pilgrims, in Lent—and all the time—use the same pattern when they pray.

Psalm 131:3

> Israel, rely on Yahweh,
> now and for always!

Matthew 6:25, 32-34

> 'That is why I am telling you not to worry
> about your life, and what you are to eat, nor
> about your body and how you are to clothe it.
> . . . Your heavenly Father knows you need
> them all. Set your hearts on his kingdom first,
> and on his righteousness, and all these other
> things will be given you as well. So do not worry
> about tomorrow: tomorrow will take care of
> itself.'

Read: Matthew 6:24-34

6.

PILGRIMS ALWAYS
TRUST THE LORD

A young Italian father, appropriately named Dante, Dante Ottaviani, thought he had lost paradise in the form of a street peddler's license to sell radios and watches near the railroad station in Rome. The authorities were willing to grant him a license to sell in a small town south of Rome, where he knew that he could not possibly earn a living as a peddler to support his wife and children, but they would not issue a license for Rome; his criminal record was against him. Dante could see no hope of making an honest living without the license he desired; he could only do two things—steal, which he had done and didn't want to do any more, or peddle watches and radios. He needed a license for that. So Dante climbed to the top of the Coliseum in the middle of a Roman winter and stayed there for over a week. He never threatened to jump; he merely wanted to advertise his plight and appeal to the local government to reverse its ruling and grant him his peddler's license. He made his point and won by trusting that his fellowmen would respond to his need if they really knew it.

Pope Paul VI makes a pilgrimage—the Stations of the Cross—to the Coliseum on Good Friday, carrying a light cross for the last few stations, and preaching a short sermon as part of the Good Friday devotions. He moves to a spot opposite the Coliseum, with the Arch of Constantine to his right and the ruins of Constantine's Basilica and the Roman Forum behind him. The place where he prays and preaches is considerably above the street which runs around the Coliseum. Had Dante Ottaviani been in his perch on the Coliseum on Good Friday, an interesting confrontation would have taken place. It could have been—as he faced the cross—as it was on another hill, "that is why I am telling you not to worry about your life, and what you are to eat, nor about your body and how you are to clothe it. . . . Your heavenly Father knows you need them all." Would he, would we, have trusted God and come down from the wall?

Life is precious and precarious

The holy pilgrimage which takes place in Lent is a response to his continuing action on our behalf and a quest for the life of his kingdom. Pilgrims experience the gifts of God which enrich their whole existence on earth. As they go up to Jerusalem, they expect their faith, hope, love, trust, and obedience to be renewed, and this happens as they rely upon God as the source and sustainer of their lives.

With our lives threatened in so many ways in this

age, the preciousness and precariousness of life are closely coupled together. Life is God's gift to man and his world, irreplaceable and incomparable, and to be cherished by the creatures made in the image of God. Three groups of young people accompanied by sponsors and three seminarians who worked at the churches they represented, set out on a winter week-end retreat. It was to be a mixture of study, social activities, skiing, and worship. Two of the groups were at the ski lodge, waiting for the third section of young people, when one of the seminarians was called to the telephone. The third seminarian spoke to him, "We won't be meeting you. There's been a terrible accident. Four of our girls and a mother have been killed." The seminarian who heard all of this said, "I was stunned—in a daze." He took the other seminarian aside with their leaders, told them what had happened, and they decided to continue the retreat as best they could, and to withhold the tragic news of the accident until they got home. Later, the seminarian said, "I had to do something." He took his skiis and went to the top of a ski trail, and went down as fast as he could, the wind and the snow flying in his face and the tragedy spinning in his mind. "I had only two clear thoughts," he explained, "How good it is to be alive, and how precarious our lives are." The young man who went to, and hung upon, a cross evokes the same kind of reaction in pilgrims who go that way, look at him suffering and dying there, and dare to think of the implications of it all. Conditions in this world intensify the effect—and our reaction.

Pilgrims appreciate life and preserve it

Once we get to the point of really perceiving how precious and precarious life is we come to that quality and level of appreciation which seeks to preserve it. The Passion and cross, rightly understood, demonstrate the high value God places upon life, and the extreme measures he goes to to preserve it. The cross is never simply another example of how temporary and tragic life really is. God chose to set up that cross in a world where life was cheap, where humanity was beset by the same types of social ills that plague us today—poverty, hunger, war, injustice, disease and illness—and for all people and all time he let it be known that life is precious to him. The cross is the sign of the value placed upon life and the symbol of his action to preserve it.

Man has to do everything in his power to sustain and preserve life on earth; that's one of the hard and clear facts of contemporary life. A major European city provides a parable in an unusual crisis that occurred there. Squatters, part of a ragged army of 60,000 poor and homeless people who keep that city under permanent siege from their shacks and lean-tos surrounding it on all sides and infiltrating it by taking over every vacant lot they can find for their hovels, launched an unusual assault. They moved in silent little groups into the city, searched out vacant apartments and homes, and moved into them.

Their "find and occupy" mission resulted in a promise from the city authorities to ready 5000 housing units in a few months. The city placed top priority upon the search for a solution to the immediate and ultimate problems of preserving the lives of the poor and making life worth living for them. The larger situation involves us all as persons whose life and existence are in jeopardy. We know that radical action to improve the future of life on earth and to insure that future is necessary. This will take all of our ingenuity, imagination, and determination.

In God we trust

Belief in Jesus and acceptance of his word do not mean that life is no longer a struggle for survival; rather, it declares that there is a point in that struggle—if it is to be successful—that we know God is on our side. In the final analysis, only God, the giver of life, can sustain it in the face of death and destruction. This is an essential part of the whole Bible, and it is highlighted by our experience at the cross. Pilgrims therefore, love the Lord and trust him with their lives!

Robert Flynn's *The Sounds of Rescue, the Signs of Hope* is a story of something that happened, during World War II when he was 11 or 12 years of age. The reader wonders, with the wealth of subjects currently available on which to base a novel, why the author chose to tell the tale of an American fighter pilot who was shot down in World War II, and managed to reach a tropical island. It is the story of a struggle for survival in that remote and isolated spot, of a man who thinks primarily about his life, the good and the bad in it in the past, and what it ought to be in the present. He writes and re-writes the survival manuals from experience, and makes all sorts of suggestions for improving them. He always hopes for rescue, but all he can do is trust and wait. As time passes, his condition deteriorates to the point where he finally admits, "I am dying"—and suddenly the story changes. God, whose name had only been an expression of profanity until that point, suddenly becomes real to him, occupies his mind. Like so many people, he says, "I never thought much about God because I never had time for anything that unimportant."

In the last 20 pages of the 270 page book, Lt. Gregory Wallace, the stranded flyer, turns his concerns and his life completely around. He says, in several different forms, "I know there is a God, and that He created me. It was He who rescued me from my mother's womb, He who lifted me out of the sea, He who saved me from despair. In His own time He will rescue me from this island. His name is the Rescue God, and above Him there is no other." When he has finally learned to look beyond his constant struggle to sustain life and his hope to regain life so that he can enjoy it, to God the source of all life, the message of the book for modern man becomes evident: ". . . I am telling you not to worry about your life and what you are to eat, nor about your body and how you are to clothe it. . . . Set your hearts on his kingdom first, and on his righteousness, and all these other things will be given you as well."

The conclusion of the novel has a strange resemblance to Good Friday, as Wallace writes his last words in the logbook: ". . . the sun is dark at midday. The sky is black and green and the sea is the color of old bronze. Everything is hushed and still and even the sea is silent.

"I tremble in excitement and expectancy. The hair rises on the back of my neck and my pulse quickens. It is the sign of the coming of the Rescue God. It is the beginning of a new day. It is the time for change."

His last words are a *maranatha* for modern man: " . . . Come Great God with lightning in your wings."

Pilgrims meet God, the sustainer of the life he provides, at the cross of Jesus Christ. There in the Passion and death of the crucified Lord we find him. And as we do, we know the value which God places on our lives—all life—and what love and trust are too. Then life is really worth living, and our struggle to preserve it is worthwhile; we can be optimistic about its outcome. We can trust him in death, as well as life—always, and in all things!

Psalm 134:1

> Come, bless Yahweh
> all you who serve Yahweh,
> serving in the house of Yahweh, . . .

Matthew 5:13-16

> 'You are the salt of the earth. But if salt be-
> comes tasteless, what can make it salty again?
> It is good for nothing. . . .
> 'You are the light of the world. A city built on
> a hilltop cannot be hid. . . . In the same way
> your light must shine in the sight of men, so
> that, seeing your good works, they may give
> praise to your Father in heaven.'

Read also: Matthew 7:15-27

7.

PILGRIMS PAY THE HIGH COST OF DISCIPLESHIP

There is a church in Europe that I have renamed, "The Church of the Cryptic Cross." At first glance, the crucifix above the altar looks like many other crucifixes—a mixture of tragedy and triumph, for the body of the dead Lord hangs there. Look more closely at cross and corpus, and a detail not usually included in such religious appointments becomes evident; the sign with the "King of the Jews" inscription on it, hanging above his head, is not straight, or securely fastened to the cross—it has torn loose at one corner and dangles from a single nail. On additional inspection, one notices that the crown of thorns has fallen off the head of the Lord, which is tilted toward the earth. The effect of this combination of details is simply to imply that the Lord had been abandoned by his followers, neglected or misrepresented by those who say they love him. It suggests to me during Lent that pilgrims pay

the high cost of discipleship by being true to him
and his word in what they say and do.

The cost of discipleship is high

As we approach the cross of Christ and the exas-
perating and exalting events of Holy Week, Good
Friday, and Easter, our lives become more complicated. We pilgrims are disciples, following the
Lord, reacting again to what is happening, reliving
the Passion as best we are able, and reflecting on
his words and deeds. We are appalled by the turn
of events after Jesus entered Jerusalem, particularly
by the ugly pattern of betrayal, denial, abandon-
ment—expressions of self-preservation—that we have
to face again in the disciples. Sensitive Christians
cannot help becoming sick at heart as the climactic
events of the Passion are remembered and reviewed.
The pattern of our own perfidy surfaces, and it is
too familiar, too repelling to be faced for very long.

Who wants to be a disciple, when the cost is so
high? Who wants to declare that Jesus is Lord, when
it may—in one way or another—cost him his life?
Jesus has established the pattern for discipleship
and it is expensive. Perhaps this is what the various
generations of our time have rejected and why the
Christian Church seems to be so dead! We want to
make our own rules about our lives and philosophies
and then we are surprised to discover that something
has gone wrong with *our* plans and *our* world.

David Ely, in a story called "The Glory of G.
O'D.," indicates that the basic problem with contemporary society and the church is that people

don't want to believe in God and obey him, they
want to be God and "do their own thing." In his
story, George O'Donnell ("G. O'D.") is a little man
who became upset by the "God is dead" theology.
He knew that it was partly an attempt to clothe
God in contemporary terminology; this he could accept. What really bothered him was that some people
really believed that God is dead. He took this per-
sonally, because, for most of his life, he had known
that George O'Donnell is God! He thought others
might have similar insights and beliefs, so he in-
serted an ad in the classified advertisements of a
newspaper:

> Anyone honestly believing himself to be God,
> kindly write full particulars to Box D 44.

The response was overwhelming; he soon had
enough mail to make his room look like a post office,
but he was afraid to open it. When he did muster
enough courage, he discovered that every person
who wrote to him believed that he was God—and
had all kinds of proof. Some included money and,
before he knew it, he accumulated more money
than he earned in a year. He was elated by the let-
ters, which were so encouraging that he decided to
do something. He checked the statistics and discovered that 93.4% of the people who had been exposed
to his ad had responded. Nearly everybody! So he
started an I-Am-God Club which became, at $5
per person, an immediate success. Soon he was
wealthy and important. He gave talks, did good
works, and built a skyscraper which he called the

God Building. He lived on top of it, in a penthouse. "The Glory of G. O'D." ends on this note:

> Often in the early evening, after a busy and fruitful day, G. O'D. (George O'Donnell) would stroll out on the balcony of his penthouse high atop the God Building, and there, full of thankfulness and contentment, he would gaze benignly down at the thousands of twinkling lights below and raise one hand in benediction.

David Ely seems to think that this, to some degree, represents every man's dream, based on the way people—Christians and non-Christians—live. God's death doesn't bother us as much as our own; we are the ones who are really important to the world.

Pilgrims are also disciples

The gospel created an I-Am-A-Disciple Club— the Christian Church—wherein there is one God and loving Father of all, one Lord and Savior, Jesus Christ. Its purpose is to gather together all the children of God through the gospel, so that he will receive the glory that is rightly his from those who inhabit his earth and receive his gifts. He is not elected to office by the membership; his kingdom is no democracy. God alone determines and makes known through his Word what he expects of the members, the believers. And the cross reminds us that even the Son, Jesus Christ, had to abide by the pattern for life detailed in that Word. The same cross calls believers—pilgrims—to true discipleship as "little Christs," servants of the living God.

The cross is a sign of hope and love to the world,

but it is a sign of confrontation to pilgrims, forcing us to test the depths and expression of our discipleship. How "salty" are we? What is our worth as Christians? How brightly and clearly does our faith shine in the world? Do we truly represent the Lord, and do we dare to be different than people who profess no belief in a living God? Lent is the time to straighten that "King of the Jews" sign above his head and put the crown back upon his brow—not only in our hearts, but in the world through our discipleship.

How pilgrims pay the high cost of discipleship

In Jesus' terms, discipleship is more than unthinking devotion or mindless dedication to the business of serving the Lord. The church must be profitable to him, as well as loyal—witness the parable of the talents—and this puts pressure upon his disciples to add imagination to their zeal, creative thought to their efforts to communicate his message to the world that God is real and his love for his children is thoroughly evident in Christ and his Passion. It is so easy to deny his existence through what one does while confessing that Jesus is Lord. And even when our intentions are the best, our faith and dedicated service firmly based on his Word, we can, unintentionally and for lack of thought, misrepresent him and prove to be unprofitable servants, even false prophets.

Peter Matthiessen's novel, *At Play in the Fields of the Lord,* is a story which causes Christians to consider their image in the light of their attempts to

serve God. Martin Quarrier and his wife leave
North Dakota, receive a limited theological training, and, filled with zeal, go to South America as
missionaries to a savage tribe that is reminiscent of
the Auca Indians of a decade or so ago. Matthiessen, an anthropologist as well as a novelist, shows
the church how ridiculous its divisions look to the
world. The resident Protestant missionary calls the
Catholic priest "the Opposition" and avoids contact
with him. Neither Catholics nor Protestants make
any deep impression according to the story, on the
lives of the people they encounter. Quarrier goes
into the interior, makes contact with the Indians,
giving them gifts like machetes with crosses carved
on the handles, and teaching them that his Jesus is
their god Kisu. But the venture fails; relationships
between him and the Indians break down, and finally
he is martyred with a cross-carved machete. Shortly
before he dies, Moon, an American Indian soldier
of fortune who has been living with the Indians, tells
him what went wrong:

". . . You taught them that the white man's God
was an angry and evil spirit (for their Kisu brought
floods during the rainy season); you asked them to
love their evil spirit."

Quarrier can only reply, "Do you realize what I
have taught these people? Not only that Jesus Christ
is evil, but that the Christian God is identical with
one of their many gods—I don't wonder the poor
fellows were confused."

It is one thing to leave the sign of the cross askew
and the crown off his head, but it is something else
to replace that sign with another that misrepresents

him—or to knock off the crown, even unintentionally as though to say, "It—He—is nothing to you, all you who pass by." It is one thing to lose our relationship with God—a tragic thing indeed, but it is utterly disastrous when, through indifference, carelessness, or thoughtlessness, we turn others away from him.

Pilgrims pay the high cost of discipleship as they straighten the "King of Kings" sign and replace Jesus' crown through truly honest and dedicated discipleship and through intelligent and thoughtful service. Then the people who hear our words and see our deeds for the kingdom will know that we really believe in God and that Jesus Christ is our Lord and King. They may just become pilgrims too and participate in the pilgrimage led by the Lord!

Psalm 133:1, 3

> How good, how delightful it is
>   for all to live together like brothers: . . .
> where Yahweh confers his blessing,
>   everlasting life.

Matthew 26:17-19

> Now on the first day of Unleavened Bread the
> disciples came to Jesus to say, 'Where do you
> want us to make the preparations for you to
> eat the passover?' 'Go to so-and-so in the city'
> he replied 'and say to him, "The Master says:
> My time is near. It is at your house that I am
> keeping Passover with my disciples."' The dis-
> ciples did what Jesus told them and prepared
> the Passover.

> Read also: Matthew 26:20-29

66

8.

A PASSION PREVIEW
FOR PILGRIMS

In a contemporary short story, a college professor receives a letter from his brother who lives with their parents on the family farm. Instinctively, he knew, despite the guarded nature of its contents, that something was wrong and that he should go home and investigate. But he didn't make the trip, and he tried to put the incident out of his mind and quiet his conscience. One day his brother visited him and, in the course of their conversation, revealed what prompted him to contact the professor; he had been having a nightmare, in which he saw himself becoming insane. It constantly recurred, growing in clarity and intensity. The professor assured his brother that he had nothing to worry about, because, as he said to him, "You don't have that kind of a mind."

Finally, after another appeal from his brother, he went home, visited with his elderly parents while awaiting his brother's return. The professor had to go to a bar to find his brother—and there they had another long conversation, dominated by his brother's obsession. Positive that he had convinced his brother that he was not going out of his mind, he took him home and they went to bed. At dawn, the blast of a shotgun almost threw him out of bed; the professor knew what had happened before he started for his brother's room. He never thought that the brother's terrible dream would have such awful and final results. After the funeral and his return to his home, he began to have the same kind of dream—and its terrifying fear. The reader knows that it is just a matter of time until the professor will take the same route to death his brother had followed.

The last meal and the final word

That Jesus and his disciples should spend a last evening together and share a final meal seems fitting indeed. He had told them again and again that his death had been prophesied in Scripture and that Scripture would be fulfilled. He had tried to prepare them for his death by stressing that his pilgrimage to Jerusalem was to be a special trip, a journey they would never forget. Hadn't he said, before they started, "Now we are going up to Jerusalem, and the Son of Man is about to be handed over to the chief priests and scribes. They will condemn him to death and will hand him over to the pagans to be mocked and scourged and crucified; and on the third day he will rise again." But they didn't really understand.

A last supper and a final word to the disciples

were necessary and desirable: "My time is near. . . . I am keeping Passover with my disciples." He needed that evening for a final review of the Passion to focus their attention on what was about to happen, and help them live through it. And so when the preparations were complete and they had gathered in the room where he had decided to celebrate the Passover meal, he washed their feet, ate the meal with them, informed them that one of them would betray him, and instituted that memorial of his death which we call the Eucharist. By the time they went to the Garden of Gethsemane, they must have been aware of—and alarmed at—what he had said was going to happen. He had given them a preview of his Passion and death!

Death with a difference

Death was Jesus' destiny. He believed that he was born to die and that this was God's plan for his life. And that is one of the most difficult things about Christianity for contemporary people to believe. Our emphasis is on living and the preservation of life on earth and we are beginning to stress service to man as the highest expression of love of life and God. The newspapers carried a story about a 48 year old mother, who is turning to a church vocation. She was almost 45 when she entered college and now she is in a Roman Catholic school. She ultimately hopes to write religious curricular materials as the expression of her faith. She told an interviewer, "I always thought there had to be more to life than there was in the way we were living it." It took her

20 years to seek a deeper faith and to probe its dimensions and implications. She is a Christian of and for her times.

Jesus went beyond the ordinary, even the inspired, conceptions of Christian service which we might hold with his "for this cause I came into the world," pushing back the earth-bound horizons of faith in God and stressing the eternal dimensions of life. He "laid down" his life, not, as we too often do, to get rid of problems, pain, or fear permanently, but so that he could "take it up" again through the power of God. Life was not too much for him; death didn't mark out its limits. Death for Jesus was part of life—that was the difference, ". . . I tell you, I shall not drink wine until the day I drink the new wine with you in the kingdom of my Father." Jesus' death on the cross became a way into the fulness of life, not a way out of it! Because death could be his destiny, life can be ours!

The Passover in new perspective

In a column "Meeting Golda Meir," William F. Buckley, Jr., calls Israel "the home of shrines," and indicates, through the last paragraph of his article, that he was a pilgrim when he was in Israel:

> I saw one day two dozen American Negro women, at the subterranean cave in the Church of the Nativity. Their preacher spontaneously delivered a little homily, and led them, then, into song. I remembered Whittaker Chambers' word about the rise of the spiritual among the Negro people, "the most God-obsessed, (and

man-despised) people since the ancient Hebrews. . . . Grief, like a tuning fork, gave the
tone, and the Sorrow Songs were uttered."
There, at Bethlehem, holding each others' hands,
they sang "Little David, Play on your Harp,"
and one senses why the term Judaeo-Christian
came to be hyphenated.

It was really at a table—not the manger—when the
Christian faith was most clearly articulated by con-
necting it to the ancient and hallowed Passover.
Without forgetting what God did in Egypt, and even
asking the question, "Why is this night different
from every other night?"—a new chapter is added:
". . . on the same night that he was betrayed, the
Lord Jesus took some bread, and thanked God, . . .
broke it, . . . and said 'This is my body, . . . do this
as a memorial of me.'" (1 Corinthians 11:23, 24).
The Passover was given the perspective of the Passion and cross.

That one night made the Passover current—in
the light of the events of the next three days—and
changed it forever! When President Nixon made his
celebrated trip to mainland China in 1972, Max
Lerner wrote that he "was trying to change twenty-
five years of history in one week." Jesus changed
thousands of years of man's history with God and
on his earth in a single night. He made deliverance
from death into a continuing action, with present
and future implications for all time. Pilgrims hence-
forth might remember with gratitude the blood of the
lambs with which the door lintels were painted in
Egypt, but they could never forget that the Lamb

of God spilled his blood on Calvary's cross that sin and death might be destroyed through him.

Love with all limits removed

The preview of the Passion, which Jesus presented to the disciples—and to all pilgrims since that night—is a revelation of the love of God with all limits removed. The Last Supper with the disciples was the beginning of a new and ongoing feast to which every person on earth is invited. The Passover was for a single people, an emerging nation, Israel. But as Jesus altered it and added his personal sacrifice to it, it became an act of deliverance for everyone from the common enemy, death.

In Jesus' life and death, God offers his love to the world, with, as Paul Scherer puts it, "both hands quite full"—of nails! Pinned there to a tree, the offer is both irrevocable and genuine. There is no mistaking his death as a sign of love and divine concern for his children. God has never disappointed, and never will disappoint, those who love and trust him! Charlotte Mandell, in Nancy Potter's story, "There Won't Be Any Scars at All," is a college student who falls in love with her professor, gets involved with him, and then, with many girls before her, is rebuffed; she cuts her wrists but survives. The professor, Dr. Pious, visits her in the hospital and says, "I was very concerned when I heard about you this morning." But Charlotte rejects him and his assertion of concern: "I have to tell you a few things." She condemns him, saying, "You were concerned about whether somebody had killed herself and about whether you should tip a head waiter and about whether you can wear your brown jacket once more before you send it to the cleaner's. I spent some time last night reflecting on your concerns," she tells him, "and I reached the conclusion that all of them are too small to be seen with the naked eyes."

At a table in an upper room, Jesus gave—and gives—a preview of the Passion and the cross, a declaration and demonstration of God's love for the world expressed through his Son. After supper, that last meal with the disciples, he left the sanctuary of the upper room to speak the final word of love from the cross. Everyone who looks at that cross can know how much God loves the world and men, and confess that "Jesus Christ is Lord, to the glory of God the Father."

Psalm 130:1, 2

> From the depths I call to you, Yahweh,
> Lord, listen to my cry for help!

Matthew 27:33-36

> When they had reached a place called Golgo-
> tha, that is, the place of the skull, they gave
> him wine to drink mixed with gall, which he
> tasted but refused to drink. When they had fin-
> ished crucifying him they shared out his cloth-
> ing by casting lots and then sat down and stayed
> there keeping guard over him. . . .

> Read also: Matthew 27:1-66

9.

THE DAY THAT PILGRIMS CAN NEVER FORGET

Good Friday was the day that Jesus' pilgrimage to Jerusalem ended the way he said it would—in disaster. Death on a cross brought an unwelcome conclusion to his crusade to initiate the kingdom of God on earth. Early that morning, a mob with clubs and swords, guided by Judas, captured Christ at Gethsemane; his disciples deserted, leaving Jesus to face his fate alone. Roman justice was swift and cruel, and after appearances before Caiaphas and the Sanhedrin, Herod and Pilate, the mockery called a trial came to an end with Pilate's sentence, "Take him out and crucify him." There and then he made his last march, forced to carry the cross on which they nailed him. He was dead in a matter of six hours. Those are the six hours the world will never forget!

Good Friday can never be forgotten

The details and drama of this sordid story create a day never to be forgotten. When Jesus died the hopes of humanity were doomed. Earth can never again be the paradise it was at the beginning—and men dream of its being again; there is no room for goodness, brotherhood, peace, and love. What Jesus taught on another hillside became forever unrealistic as he hung on the cross:

> How happy are the poor in spirit;
> theirs is the kingdom of heaven.
> Happy the gentle;
> they shall have the earth for their heritage.
> Happy those who mourn. . . .
> Happy those who hunger and thirst for what is
> right. . . .
> Happy the pure in heart. . . .
> Happy the peacemakers. . . .
> Happy those who are persecuted in the cause of
> right. . . .

On Good Friday, these are the words of a dreamer, a man deluded by a vision of a God-like kingdom on earth, inhabited by people who actually live like children of God. For this is the day when man who had been snarling and snapping at God since the creation, finally bit the gracious hand of God like a dog. Made in God's own image, man prefers to live like a savage animal.

The day of Jesus' death can't be forgotten; it is the day when everyone is sentenced to death again. Death is inescapable, unconquerable, if the Son of God must die like everyone else, and man is but like every other form of life. Death takes on a grim and grotesque quality that etches an indelible impression on the spirit of man. It is like taking a tour through the catacombs of Rome; most of them have been tidied up so that they are interesting, but sterile. One catacomb tour, that of St. Calixtus, is different from all the others, because at the end of it, visitors are taken into a small room where there are two glass-covered stone caskets over 1600 years old, which contain all this is left of two 4th century Christians. Perhaps it is the setting—after all, seeing human remains is a universal and common experience—but people are obviously shaken by what they see; many take one glance and hurry out of the tombs. The Christ on the cross leaves man no place to go to escape from death and his fear of it.

The death of Jesus can't be forgotten. It leaves all the old questions about life after death, which insistently haunt people, unanswered or vague. Tillie Seltzer, in Peter DeVries' novel, *Witch's Milk*, reacts typically to the death of her nine year old son, Charlie, asking herself and her less-intellectual husband Pete, all the "why's?" Desperate for a small measure of comfort at least, she asks Pete:

"Will I see Charlie again?"

He attempts to reassure her: "Of course you will." But his arguments are weak: "There's a lot of new evidence about that. That the societies for psychical research and all are getting. You never know. We don't know anything. I was reading the other day where astronomers have discovered some strange blue particles in the Milky Way they didn't know were there. So cheer up."

Pete's final words, held up against man's eternal experience with death, are weak and pale in the face of the cross and the immediacy of Charlie's death: "I mean if nothing is certain, then everything

is possible. The whole universe is mysteries to be
unlocked, if we can swing it, and I think we can.
. . . So buck up." Better to be a Stoic, forget the
questions about death and simply live, "Let us eat,
drink, and be merry, for tomorrow we die." Good
Friday is but Jesus' turn to die, pathetic and regret-
table, but the common fate of all men, and we are
next!

A Day that must be remembered

But those are not our reasons for calling Good
Friday "a day that can never be forgotten." If they
were, we wouldn't call it "good"; we'd rename it
something like "Black Friday"—the day when the
world began to come to an end. We believe that
God had something to do with those horrible, de-
grading events that gives radiance and glory to
them and transforms that tragedy into a triumph
for him and his kingdom. The Apostle Paul speaks
for us, "God was in Christ, reconciling the world
unto himself," and we take our stand with him!

That doesn't make it all less puzzling or painful.
Faith doesn't mean that we can bypass death and
the hurt of it, any more than could God, if he were
to save the world. Toward the end of 1971, a man
named Joseph Kramer presented a parchment scroll,
the Torah, to a congregation in Tel Aviv. The scroll
was a memorial for the 18 month old son that Kramer
had smothered to death in order to save the lives
of 47 Jews who were being hunted down by the
Nazis in 1943. Yitzah Nimtsovitz, the journalist who
learned the story and was present at the dedication

of the scroll, wrote: "This man's anguish cannot be imagined. . . . He was hysterical with grief." Nimtsovitz tells how Kramer, his wife Genia, and their son, David, lived in the village of Dolhinov, in Latvia. There he had built a bunker under his house which sheltered his family and 45 other Jews from the Nazis. David began to cry when the soldiers approached the bunker, and became hysterical when Kramer tried to quiet him: "All eyes in the bunker turned on Kramer. For a long anguished time he tried to smother the child's cries, and then he took the only possible action. He smothered his son to save their lives. All the Jews in the bunker escaped, and some were present in Tel Aviv the day that the scroll was presented by Kramer to the Ramat Yosef Synagogue.

God *was* there when they crucified his Son at Calvary, not standing by impotently, unable to do anything, but suffering as only the loving Father could suffer, far more than anyone else. Perhaps we can at best only begin to understand the depth of God's painful dilemma, but we can comprehend that Jesus' death was in our best interests. The death of Jesus on a cross can't be forgotten; it means life and salvation to us all. Good Friday is a day that is remembered by everyone who has heard the wonderful story of the Son of God who died then and there for all mankind.

The Day when pilgrims gather again

Good Friday is celebrated by an evergrowing community of the faithful, which makes the annual pilgrimage to Jerusalem and Golgotha, comprehending enough of that mysterious action to perceive that the cross is the emblem of man's hope. The death of Jesus is the beginning of a new era for the whole human race. A new dimension has been added to man's problem with physical death; now there is the promise of an answer, new life! "As in Adam all die, so in Christ shall all be made alive."

Going through the experience of death is still necessary and painful, but this we know: Death may claim us, but it cannot hold us, thanks to God and Jesus' death on our behalf. The mystery and many of the questions still persist, but we stand firm in the belief that God picked up the pieces of a world that was broken into bits on a day called Good Friday and made all things new again three days later.

Good Friday is the day that Christians will never forget. It is the day that Jesus calls upon his pilgrims, who have "gone up to Jerusalem" with him again, to gather and regroup at his cross and follow him as he makes his final assault on sin and death. In reverence and devotion, we, the gathered pilgrims, pause to ponder his death on the cross once more. Then we move to his grave, the empty tomb, where we really learn what the pilgrimage is all about: "He is not here. He is risen, as He said." The prophets were right! "Thanks be to God who gives us the victory in Jesus Christ through his cross!"

Psalm 126:1, 2, 5, 6

> When Yahweh brought Zion's captives home,
>   at first it seemed like a dream;
> then our mouths were filled with laughter
>   and our lips with song.
> . . . .
> Those who went sowing in tears
>   now sing as they reap.
> They went away, went away weeping,
>   carrying the seed;
> they come back, come back singing,
>   carrying their sheaves.

Matthew 20:19

> " . . . and on the third day he will rise again."

> Read also: Matthew 28:1-10

10.

POSTSCRIPT TO THE PASSION: PILGRIMS AGAIN

Dawn on that day we now call Easter saw a sad looking group of pilgrims passing out the city gate. Just a few women were left of the pilgrim band that Jesus had led to Jerusalem. Their heads were held high, not because they were brave or proud, but because they carried jars and pots with spices and precious ointments in them for their final act of love to Jesus. They seemed to float gracefully over the ground, but each woman felt that her feet were dragging; every step was an effort. They didn't talk, but their faces eloquently expressed their sorrow and their unspoken anxiety. They still had two problems: how to get past the guards, and how to move the stone from the entrance to the tomb; they knew they could expect no help from the Roman soldiers.

The short journey seemed to take forever. But, suddenly, as they entered Joseph's garden, an earthquake shook them out of their private worlds of grief and thought into reality once more. They knew immediately that they were up against the unexpected again, and they were afraid that their plans might be upset. Mary of Magdala hurried to the tomb and discovered that their problems were solved: the guards were nowhere to be seen, and the stone had been rolled from the tomb—it was open, an invitation to enter. And then they had a greater problem, the predicament that everyone faces when he hears the news of Easter, as a messenger from God said: "There is no need for you to be afraid. I know you are looking for Jesus, who was crucified. He is not here, for he has risen, as he said he would. Come and see the place where he lay, then go quickly and tell his disciples, 'He has risen from the dead....'"

Easter gave pilgrims a new alternative

The crucifixion of Jesus Christ left the pilgrims who had gone up to Jerusalem with him with two choices: they could express their love by finishing the embalming process and going back home to try to salvage something from their experiences with Jesus; or they could give in to despair and forget about the God who allowed their whole world to cave in on them. Easter gave them another alternative just as it does us today: Dare we believe that Jesus is really alive again, that he has conquered death as well as sin, and that he is actually Lord of the living and the dead?

The news of Easter sets us to singing:

> Christ the Lord is risen today,
> Sons of men and angels say;
> Raise your joys and triumphs high,
> Sing, ye heavens, and earth, reply.
> Vain the stone, the watch, the seal;
> Christ hath burst the gates of hell;
> Death in vain forbids his rise,
> Christ hath opened Paradise.
>
> (Charles Wesley—SBH, #91)

It isn't too difficult to sing hymns like that—they may even thrill us on Easter morning—but it is something else really to believe what we sing! The Easter message is the very heart of the gospel and it always will be difficult to believe. The choice of believing or rejecting the angel's word, "He is not here, he is risen, as he said" is the alternative that Easter offers; and the choice must be made!

Alternatives to Easter

Easter's perplexing and mysterious alternative—Jesus' resurrection and what this means—sends people scurrying to discover alternatives to Easter. The kind of scientific world we live in prompts us to find another solution than resurrection to the problem of death. Cryogenics, quick-freezing of human bodies at death like we freeze vegetables and meat, is a viable option for some people today. One wonders whether Robert P. Eaton's assertion about billionaire Howard Hughes—that he is "seeking an alternative to death" and has studied cryogenics and a "realistic method" to achieve "eventual revival after he dies"—is true. Will cyrogenics give him and other moderns a better solution to death than resurrection, or will it create, simply, more questions? "Will it work?"; "How can we be sure that someone in the future will want to revive us?"; and, "How can we have any assurance that the world will be better in the future than it is now?" are questions we have to ask. And, ultimately, death will have to be faced; life can't go on forever! Science will never be the source of eternal life.

The intelligent alternative to Easter is to accept Jesus' ethical and moral teachings, even his sacrificial death on the cross as an example of what love ought to be like, and settle for these as gospel. But this approach, or any variation of it which eliminates the resurrection or twists it out of shape, won't do either. This alternative limits God's power and every semblance of divine mystery; man is pretty much on his own when Easter is eliminated or deemphasized. That leaves Jesus as just another man, an example to be emulated, but something less than Lord. A gospel without the resurrection is no gospel at all, simply because the authority of his Word and the meaning of the cross are lost.

Easter generates acceptance of the cross

Louis Cassels, religion columnist for the UPI, once wrote at Easter: "Jesus confronts us today, not as a memory out of the past, but as a present fact and challenge." As risen Lord Jesus is the present Christ, alive and active, and Lord of heaven and earth. Not only has he, through God's power, defeated death, but sin has really been destroyed; its hold is broken forever. God and his love have triumphed over all the destructive forces of evil. Robert Nathan pictures, in his *The Devil with Love,* a discussion in hell between Beelzebub and Lucifer. Beelzebub accuses Lucifer of loving Christ, but he denies it.

Later on in the conversation, Lucifer remarks: "It is much easier to hate than to love. . . . To hate is to exclude, to love is to accept, to draw in . . . which calls for a different set of muscles. To say No is to finish something; to say Yes is to begin it. I wish I had hearts to love me, on earth."

At that, one of the "Shades" of hell stepped forward and said to Lucifer, "Sieg Heil!"

"Heil," said Lucifer.

"My leader," cried the shade. "Let us not bother our heads about love, which is only for cowards and Jews! We are all heroes here. Hate! That is the thing! Let us have our hearts filled with hate, as we had at home."

'So saying, he stepped back, with a satisfied air. "Thank you, Adolph," said Lucifer.

"It is nothing."

"No," admitted Lucifer sadly, "it is nothing." '

That's what the cross and resurrection accomplished!

Love is the accepted way of living in the world where Christ is the living Lord. He gives us courage to face and embrace the cross, where life and love were spilled out, and live sacrificially and lovingly on earth. Not God's Law, but Christ's love takes over in us, and with the German theologian, Willi Marxen, we can say: "I take the risk of doing what he asks, contrary to all human reason . . . at the very point where I let myself go, I discover that I am being held by something outside myself. Once I wanted to live, but could not do so. Now I give up the attempt to live, in the sense in which I have hitherto understood living, and discover that now, suddenly, I am really living."

That's what Easter does, the news that "He is risen, as he said." We die with him—at the cross, in baptism—and rise with him—through his Word, the gospel. And to all who believe that the Christ, who died at Calvary—on a cross, is the risen Lord, he says, "Come, let us go into the world—to love and serve!" And we are pilgrims again—forever!